EMMANUEL JOSEPH

Invisible Bridges: How Silence and Stillness Create Powerful Connections

Copyright © 2025 by Emmanuel Joseph

All rights reserved. No part of this publication may be reproduced, stored or transmitted in any form or by any means, electronic, mechanical, photocopying, recording, scanning, or otherwise without written permission from the publisher. It is illegal to copy this book, post it to a website, or distribute it by any other means without permission.

First edition

*This book was professionally typeset on Reedsy.
Find out more at reedsy.com*

Contents

1	Chapter 1	1
2	Chapter 1: The Quiet Revolution	2
3	Chapter 2: The Art of Silence	5
4	Chapter 3: Stillness and Mindfulness	8
5	Chapter 4: The Science of Silence	11
6	Chapter 5: Deepening Personal Relationships	13
7	Chapter 6: Professional Growth through Stillness	16
8	Chapter 7: Emotional Resilience and Silence	19
9	Chapter 8: Creative Inspiration from Stillness	22
10	Chapter 9: The Healing Power of Quietude	25
11	Chapter 10: Building a Practice of Silence	28
12	Chapter 11: Silence in Modern Society	31
13	Chapter 12: The Future of Silence	34
14	Chapter 13: 10 reflective exercises that can help you...	36

Chapter 1

Invisible Bridges: How Silence and Stillness Create Powerful Connections

2

Chapter 1: The Quiet Revolution

In a world overwhelmed by noise and constant activity, the value of silence and stillness is often overlooked. This chapter introduces readers to the concept of the "Quiet Revolution," a growing movement that recognizes the importance of disconnecting from the cacophony of modern life to reconnect with our inner selves and with others on a deeper level.

We begin by exploring the historical and cultural perspectives on silence and stillness. From ancient monastic traditions to contemporary mindfulness practices, various cultures have long understood the power of quietude. Silence is not merely the absence of sound but a state of being that fosters introspection, clarity, and profound connection. The Quiet Revolution challenges the prevailing notion that busyness equates to productivity, advocating instead for the rejuvenative power of silence.

Modern life often equates busyness with productivity, yet constant activity can lead to burnout and disconnection. Rediscovering silence can provide opportunities for self-awareness and growth. This section delves into practical ways to incorporate silence into daily routines, such as morning meditations, peaceful walks, or simply sitting quietly. These moments of quiet can rejuvenate our minds and spirits, offering a sanctuary from the

CHAPTER 1: THE QUIET REVOLUTION

relentless pace of everyday life.

Silence offers a unique opportunity to turn inward and reflect. By embracing quiet moments, we allow ourselves to process thoughts and emotions that often get buried in the hustle and bustle of daily life. This internal dialogue can lead to greater self-awareness, emotional regulation, and personal growth. The impact of silence on our mental health and well-being cannot be overstated, as it allows us to reconnect with our inner selves.

Effective communication often involves more listening than speaking. Silence creates space for deeper connections, allowing us to truly hear and understand others. In an argument, a moment of silence can defuse tension and open the door to empathetic dialogue. In a conversation, a thoughtful pause can convey respect and attentiveness. This chapter explores how embracing silence can enhance our personal relationships.

Case Study: The Power of Quiet Reflection

Meet Sarah, a high-achieving professional who found herself on the brink of burnout. Between her demanding job and social commitments, she barely had a moment to herself. Her mind was constantly racing, and she felt disconnected from her own thoughts and feelings. In search of a solution, Sarah decided to incorporate daily moments of silence into her routine. She started with just five minutes each morning, sitting quietly with her thoughts before the rush of the day began. Gradually, she extended this practice, finding solace in the early hours when the world was still.

As Sarah embraced these quiet moments, she noticed profound changes. The silence allowed her to reflect on her goals, reassess her priorities, and reconnect with her passions. She became more attuned to her emotions, recognizing the sources of her stress and finding healthier ways to cope. Over time, Sarah's practice of silent reflection led to significant personal growth. She made conscious decisions to reduce her workload, prioritize self-care, and cultivate meaningful relationships. The quiet moments became a sanctuary where she could recharge, gain clarity, and foster a deeper connection with herself.

3

Chapter 2: The Art of Silence

Silence is not merely the absence of noise; it is a profound state that transcends words and sounds. This chapter delves into the historical and cultural significance of silence, exploring how various traditions have embraced and honored quietude. We begin by examining the concept of silence in different cultures and how it has been revered and practiced over time.

Throughout history, different cultures have found unique ways to appreciate and incorporate silence into their lives. In Japan, the concept of "ma" () represents the space between sounds and words, highlighting the beauty and significance of pauses. This idea permeates many aspects of Japanese culture, from traditional tea ceremonies to modern architecture, where the balance of silence and sound creates harmony and peace. Similarly, in Quaker meetings, silence plays a central role. Quakers believe that silent worship allows individuals to listen to the "still, small voice" within, fostering a deep and personal connection with the divine. This practice of communal silence creates a space for reflection, contemplation, and shared spiritual experiences.

Cultural Reverence for Silence

Different cultures have unique ways of embracing silence. For instance, the Desert Fathers, early Christian monks, sought solitude and silence in the deserts of Egypt to deepen their spiritual practice. The Sufi mystics of Islam value silent meditation as a means of achieving union with the divine. Native American traditions also emphasize the importance of silence, viewing it as a way to connect with nature and the spiritual world. This section explores how different societies find meaning in quietude and how we can learn from these practices.

The Power of Ritual Silence

Rituals that incorporate silence can be transformative, providing moments of stillness in our busy lives. In this section, we explore various practices that emphasize the power of ritual silence, such as meditation, silent retreats, and mindful walking. These practices allow us to create intentional spaces for silence, fostering a sense of inner peace and clarity. Ritual silence can also enhance our spiritual and emotional well-being, offering a sanctuary from the noise and distractions of daily life.

Case Study: The Transformative Power of Silent Retreats

Consider the story of John, a business executive who felt overwhelmed by the constant demands of his job. Seeking respite, he attended a week-long silent retreat. At first, the silence was unsettling, but as the days passed, John began to embrace the quiet. He found that the absence of external noise allowed him to confront his inner turmoil and gain clarity on his life's direction. By the end of the retreat, John felt a renewed sense of purpose and peace. He realized that silence was not an empty void but a space filled with potential for self-discovery and healing. This experience inspired him to integrate moments of silence into his daily routine, leading to lasting positive changes in his personal and professional life.

Silent Practices for Daily Life

CHAPTER 2: THE ART OF SILENCE

Incorporating silence into daily life can be as simple as creating quiet rituals. This section provides practical advice for incorporating silence into daily routines, such as morning meditations, silent retreats, and quiet walks in nature. These practices can help us cultivate a deeper connection with ourselves and the world around us. By creating intentional spaces for silence, we can foster a sense of inner peace and clarity, enhancing our overall well-being.

4

Chapter 3: Stillness and Mindfulness

Mindfulness and stillness are intricately connected, offering a path to a more present and intentional way of living. This chapter delves into the relationship between stillness and mindfulness, exploring how moments of quiet can lead to greater awareness and tranquility.

Cultivating Mindful Stillness

Mindful practices, such as breathing exercises and body scans, can help cultivate a state of stillness. By focusing on the present moment and letting go of distractions, we can achieve a deeper sense of peace and clarity. This section provides practical techniques for integrating mindful stillness into daily life. Regular mindfulness practices can help calm the mind, reduce stress, and enhance overall well-being.

The Power of Presence

Being fully present in the moment allows us to appreciate the richness of our experiences. This section explores how stillness can enhance our ability to be present, leading to more meaningful and fulfilling interactions with the world around us. By slowing down and embracing stillness, we create space

CHAPTER 3: STILLNESS AND MINDFULNESS

for deeper connections and greater awareness of our surroundings.

Mindful Breathing Techniques

Mindful breathing is a simple yet powerful practice that can anchor us in the present moment. This section offers step-by-step instructions for mindful breathing exercises, helping readers to cultivate a sense of stillness and calm. Techniques such as deep belly breathing and focused breathing can be easily incorporated into daily routines.

Case Study: The Impact of Mindful Breathing

Meet Emily, a university student struggling with anxiety and stress. She discovered mindful breathing through a campus workshop and decided to incorporate it into her routine. By setting aside a few minutes each day to focus on her breath, Emily found herself feeling calmer and more centered. This simple practice allowed her to approach challenges with a clear mind and a steady heart, demonstrating the profound impact of mindful stillness.

Practical Applications of Mindfulness

Mindfulness can be practiced in various aspects of daily life, from eating mindfully to mindful walking. This section explores practical ways to integrate mindfulness into everyday activities, enhancing our ability to be present and fully engaged. By bringing mindfulness into our daily routines, we can create a more balanced and peaceful life.

Building a Mindfulness Practice

Developing a consistent mindfulness practice requires commitment and intention. This section offers tips and advice for building a sustainable mindfulness routine, including setting aside dedicated time for practice and creating a supportive environment. By making mindfulness a regular part of our lives, we can cultivate lasting inner peace and resilience.

Chapter 4: The Science of Silence

Silence and stillness have profound effects on our mental and physical health, as supported by scientific research. This chapter delves into the science behind the benefits of silence, exploring how quiet environments impact the brain, reduce stress, and enhance overall well-being.

The Brain on Silence

Studies have shown that periods of silence can lead to significant changes in the brain. For instance, research indicates that silence can stimulate the growth of new brain cells in the hippocampus, a region associated with memory, emotion, and learning. This section explores the neurobiological effects of silence and how it can improve cognitive functions.

Reducing Stress through Silence

Silence has a calming effect on the nervous system, helping to reduce stress levels. This section examines how quiet environments lower cortisol levels, the body's primary stress hormone, and promote a state of relaxation. We also discuss how silence can lead to lower blood pressure and improved cardiovascular health.

Enhancing Focus and Creativity

Silence can enhance our ability to focus and boost creativity. This section explores studies that show how quiet environments can improve concentration, problem-solving skills, and creative thinking. By minimizing distractions, silence allows the brain to process information more deeply and generate innovative ideas.

Case Study: The Creative Power of Silence

Consider the story of Maria, a writer who struggled with creative blocks. She decided to retreat to a remote cabin for a week of silence, hoping to rekindle her inspiration. Without the usual distractions, Maria found herself immersed in her thoughts, allowing her mind to wander freely. By the end of the week, she had written several chapters of her novel and developed new story ideas. This experience demonstrated the power of silence in fostering creativity and focus.

Silence and Emotional Regulation

Silence provides a space for emotional processing and regulation. This section explores how quiet moments allow individuals to reflect on their emotions, gain insights, and develop healthier coping mechanisms. By embracing silence, we can better understand and manage our emotional responses.

Practical Applications of Silence

Incorporating silence into daily life can be beneficial for mental and physical health. This section offers practical tips for creating quiet spaces, such as setting aside specific times for silence, reducing ambient noise, and finding peaceful environments. By intentionally incorporating silence into our routines, we can enhance our well-being and overall quality of life.

6

Chapter 5: Deepening Personal Relationships

Silence can be a powerful tool for deepening personal relationships. While words are essential for communication, silence often speaks volumes. This chapter explores how moments of quiet can enhance communication and intimacy, allowing individuals to connect on a deeper level.

The Role of Silence in Communication

Effective communication often involves more listening than speaking. Silence creates space for deeper connections, allowing us to truly hear and understand others. This section discusses how silence can foster empathy and attentiveness, leading to more meaningful interactions. By allowing moments of silence in conversations, we give ourselves and others time to process thoughts and feelings, resulting in more thoughtful and considered responses.

Silence as a Sign of Respect

INVISIBLE BRIDGES: HOW SILENCE AND STILLNESS CREATE POWERFUL CONNECTIONS

In many cultures, silence is seen as a sign of respect and attentiveness. This section explores cultural attitudes towards silence and how it can enhance our interactions with others. By being comfortable with silence, we show that we value the other person's presence and are fully engaged in the moment. This practice can build trust and mutual respect in relationships.

The Power of Listening

Active listening involves more than just hearing words; it requires us to be fully present and attentive. This section highlights the importance of active listening and how silence can create space for others to express themselves. By listening attentively and allowing silence to fill the gaps, we can better understand and connect with our loved ones.

Case Study: Strengthening Bonds through Silence

Consider the story of Tom and Lisa, a couple who found themselves drifting apart due to the demands of their busy lives. They decided to set aside a few minutes each day to sit in silence together, simply holding hands and being present with one another. This practice allowed them to reconnect on a deeper level, strengthening their bond and improving their communication. By embracing silence, they were able to listen to each other more deeply and understand each other's needs and feelings.

Using Silence to Resolve Conflicts

Silence can be a powerful tool for resolving conflicts. This section discusses how taking a moment of silence during disagreements can defuse tension and create space for empathetic dialogue. By pausing to reflect before responding, we can approach conflicts with a calmer and more open mindset, leading to more constructive resolutions.

Practical Tips for Embracing Silence in Relationships

CHAPTER 5: DEEPENING PERSONAL RELATIONSHIPS

Incorporating silence into relationships requires practice and intention. This section offers practical tips for creating quiet moments with loved ones, such as setting aside time for silent walks, meditations, or simply sitting together in silence. By making space for silence, we can deepen our connections and build stronger, more resilient relationships.

7

Chapter 6: Professional Growth through Stillness

In the workplace, moments of stillness can lead to creative breakthroughs and better decision-making. This chapter discusses how integrating stillness into professional routines can enhance productivity and innovation, providing a competitive edge in a fast-paced world.

The Role of Stillness in Creativity

Creativity often flourishes in moments of stillness. This section explores how taking time to pause and reflect can lead to innovative ideas and solutions. By creating space for quiet contemplation, professionals can tap into their creative potential and approach challenges with fresh perspectives.

Enhancing Decision-Making through Quiet Reflection

Silence and stillness can improve decision-making by allowing individuals to process information more thoroughly. This section examines how moments of quiet can lead to more thoughtful and informed decisions, reducing impulsivity and fostering better judgment. By incorporating stillness into decision-making processes, professionals can enhance their strategic thinking and problem-solving abilities.

Creating Calm Workspaces

A calm and quiet workspace can significantly impact productivity and well-being. This section offers practical tips for creating a serene work environment, such as minimizing noise, incorporating natural elements, and setting aside dedicated quiet time. By cultivating a peaceful workspace, individuals can enhance their focus and reduce stress.

Case Study: Innovation through Stillness

Consider the story of Michael, a product manager at a tech company. Facing a creative block, Michael decided to incorporate moments of stillness into his workday. He set aside time each morning for quiet reflection, allowing his mind to wander freely. During these moments, Michael often found innovative solutions and new ideas for his projects. This practice not only boosted his creativity but also improved his overall job performance. Michael's experience highlights the power of stillness in fostering professional growth and innovation.

Integrating Stillness into Work Routines

Incorporating stillness into work routines can enhance productivity and well-being. This section offers practical strategies for integrating moments of quiet into the workday, such as taking short breaks for mindfulness, practicing deep breathing exercises, and setting boundaries to reduce distractions. By prioritizing stillness, professionals can improve their focus and resilience.

The Future of Work and Stillness

As the workplace continues to evolve, the importance of stillness and quiet reflection will become increasingly recognized. This section explores the potential for incorporating stillness into the future of work, envisioning a world where quiet moments are valued and integrated into professional practices. By embracing stillness, we can create a more balanced and innovative work environment.

8

Chapter 7: Emotional Resilience and Silence

Building emotional resilience often involves embracing silence. This chapter explores how quiet reflection can help individuals process emotions, develop coping strategies, and build inner strength. Silence provides a unique opportunity to turn inward, allowing us to confront our emotions and gain insights into our emotional landscape.

The Role of Silence in Emotional Processing

Silence offers a space for emotional processing, allowing us to sit with our feelings and reflect on their origins and meanings. This section discusses how moments of quiet can help us understand and navigate our emotions, leading to greater emotional resilience. By embracing silence, we can develop a deeper understanding of our emotional responses and learn to manage them more effectively.

Cultivating Inner Strength through Silence

Silence can be a powerful tool for building inner strength and resilience. This section explores how quiet reflection can help us develop coping strategies and build emotional fortitude. By creating space for silence, we can confront our challenges with greater clarity and confidence, fostering a sense of inner strength and resilience.

The Healing Power of Quietude

Silence can contribute to emotional healing by providing a space for reflection and introspection. This section discusses how quiet moments can help us process past experiences, release negative emotions, and foster a sense of peace and acceptance. By embracing silence, we can support our emotional well-being and promote healing.

Case Study: Finding Strength in Silence

Meet David, a man who experienced a significant loss and struggled to cope with his grief. Seeking solace, he began to incorporate moments of silence into his daily routine. By setting aside time for quiet reflection, David was able to process his emotions and find a sense of peace. Over time, he developed a deeper understanding of his grief and found the strength to move forward. David's story illustrates the healing power of silence and its role in building emotional resilience.

Practical Exercises for Emotional Resilience

Incorporating silence into daily life can enhance emotional resilience. This section offers practical exercises for building emotional strength through quiet reflection, such as journaling, meditation, and mindful breathing. By making space for silence, we can develop healthier coping mechanisms and foster emotional well-being.

Creating a Supportive Environment for Silence

CHAPTER 7: EMOTIONAL RESILIENCE AND SILENCE

Creating a supportive environment for silence can enhance our emotional resilience. This section provides tips for creating quiet spaces, such as setting aside dedicated time for reflection, reducing distractions, and finding peaceful environments. By prioritizing silence, we can support our emotional well-being and build resilience.

Chapter 8: Creative Inspiration from Stillness

Artists, writers, and musicians often find inspiration in stillness. This chapter highlights how creative individuals use quiet moments to fuel their work. Silence and stillness provide a space for the mind to wander freely, allowing creative ideas to emerge without the constraints of constant noise and distractions.

The Role of Stillness in Creativity

Stillness allows the mind to enter a state of flow, where creative ideas can flourish. This section explores how moments of quiet can enhance creative thinking and lead to artistic breakthroughs. By creating space for stillness, artists can tap into their inner creativity and find inspiration in unexpected places.

Finding Inspiration in Nature

Nature often serves as a profound source of inspiration for creative individuals. This section discusses how spending time in natural settings can inspire creativity and foster a sense of stillness. By immersing ourselves in the beauty of nature, we can connect with our surroundings and draw inspiration from the world around us.

The Quiet Muse

Silence can serve as a muse, allowing creative individuals to access their inner worlds and explore new ideas. This section delves into the concept of the "quiet muse," highlighting how silence can spark creativity and innovation. By embracing stillness, artists can unlock new dimensions of their creative potential.

Case Study: The Creative Power of Stillness

Consider the story of Elena, a painter who struggled with creative blocks. Seeking a way to reignite her inspiration, she decided to spend a week in a remote cabin, surrounded by nature. Without the usual distractions, Elena found herself immersed in her thoughts and the natural beauty around her. The stillness allowed her to explore new artistic ideas and techniques, leading to a series of innovative paintings. Elena's experience demonstrates how stillness can fuel creativity and lead to artistic breakthroughs.

Practical Exercises for Tapping into Creative Potential

Incorporating stillness into daily life can enhance creativity. This section offers practical exercises for tapping into creative potential through quiet contemplation, such as mindful observation, journaling, and meditation. By making space for stillness, we can cultivate a more fertile environment for creative inspiration.

Creating a Quiet Space for Creativity

Creating a dedicated space for quiet reflection can enhance our creative

INVISIBLE BRIDGES: HOW SILENCE AND STILLNESS CREATE POWERFUL CONNECTIONS

processes. This section provides tips for setting up a quiet and inspiring workspace, such as minimizing distractions, incorporating natural elements, and creating a calming atmosphere. By fostering a serene environment, we can nurture our creative potential and find inspiration in the quiet moments.

10

Chapter 9: The Healing Power of Quietude

Silence and stillness can play a significant role in emotional and physical healing. This chapter discusses how quiet environments and practices can promote healing and well-being. By creating spaces for silence, we allow ourselves to tune into our bodies and minds, facilitating the healing process.

The Therapeutic Effects of Silence

Silence has been used as a therapeutic tool in various healing practices. This section explores how quiet environments can reduce stress, lower blood pressure, and promote relaxation. By minimizing external noise, we create a peaceful atmosphere that supports the body's natural healing processes.

Healing through Meditation and Yoga

Meditation and yoga are practices that emphasize the power of silence and stillness. This section discusses how these practices can promote physical and emotional healing. Through mindful movement and quiet reflection, we can release tension, reduce stress, and enhance our overall well-being.

The Role of Silence in Mental Health

Silence can have a profound impact on mental health, offering a space for introspection and emotional processing. This section explores how quiet moments can help individuals manage anxiety, depression, and other mental health challenges. By embracing silence, we create an environment that supports mental and emotional healing.

Case Study: The Healing Journey of Quiet Reflection

Meet Laura, a woman who experienced chronic pain and emotional distress. Seeking relief, she began to incorporate moments of silence into her daily routine. Through meditation and quiet reflection, Laura found a sense of peace and comfort. The silence allowed her to connect with her body and mind, facilitating her healing journey. Over time, she noticed significant improvements in her physical and emotional health. Laura's story highlights the healing power of quietude and its role in promoting well-being.

Practical Exercises for Healing through Silence

Incorporating silence into daily life can enhance the healing process. This section offers practical exercises for promoting healing through quiet reflection, such as guided meditations, deep breathing exercises, and mindful movement. By making space for silence, we can support our physical and emotional well-being.

Creating Healing Spaces

Creating a healing environment involves designing spaces that promote silence and stillness. This section provides tips for setting up quiet and peaceful spaces in our homes, such as creating a meditation corner, reducing clutter, and incorporating calming elements like plants and soft lighting. By fostering a serene atmosphere, we can enhance our healing journey and promote overall well-being.

11

Chapter 10: Building a Practice of Silence

Incorporating silence and stillness into daily life requires intentional practice. This chapter offers practical advice for creating routines and environments that promote quietude. By making space for silence, we can enhance our well-being and cultivate a deeper connection with ourselves and others.

Creating Quiet Rituals

Building a practice of silence involves creating intentional rituals. This section provides practical advice for incorporating silence into daily routines, such as morning meditations, silent retreats, and quiet walks in nature. These practices can help us cultivate a sense of inner peace and clarity, enhancing our overall well-being.

Establishing a Daily Routine

Consistency is key to building a practice of silence. This section offers tips for establishing a daily routine that incorporates moments of quiet, such as setting aside specific times for reflection, creating a dedicated space for meditation, and minimizing distractions. By prioritizing silence, we can

CHAPTER 10: BUILDING A PRACTICE OF SILENCE

create a sustainable and fulfilling practice.

The Benefits of Morning Silence

Starting the day with moments of silence can set a positive tone for the rest of the day. This section explores the benefits of morning silence, such as increased focus, reduced stress, and enhanced emotional regulation. By beginning the day with quiet reflection, we can approach our tasks with greater clarity and intention.

Case Study: Morning Silence for Mental Clarity

Consider the story of Lisa, a busy professional who felt overwhelmed by the demands of her job and personal life. Seeking a way to find balance, she began to incorporate moments of silence into her morning routine. By setting aside ten minutes each morning for quiet meditation, Lisa noticed significant improvements in her mental clarity and emotional well-being. This practice allowed her to approach her day with a sense of calm and focus, demonstrating the benefits of morning silence.

Creating Quiet Spaces at Home

Creating quiet spaces in our homes can enhance our practice of silence. This section offers practical tips for setting up peaceful environments, such as reducing noise, incorporating natural elements, and creating a calming atmosphere. By designing spaces that promote quietude, we can foster a sense of inner peace and well-being.

Embracing Silence in Social Settings

Incorporating silence into social settings can deepen our connections with others. This section explores ways to embrace silence in social interactions, such as practicing mindful listening, allowing for pauses in conversation, and engaging in silent activities together. By making space for silence, we can enhance our relationships and foster more meaningful connections.

12

Chapter 11: Silence in Modern Society

Embracing silence in a technology-driven world can be challenging yet rewarding. This chapter reflects on the societal shifts towards valuing quiet spaces and moments. As we navigate the constant barrage of information and noise, finding time for silence becomes increasingly important for our well-being and mental health.

The Impact of Technology on Silence

Technology has revolutionized the way we communicate and interact, but it has also introduced new challenges to finding moments of silence. This section explores the impact of technology on our ability to experience quietude, highlighting the constant presence of digital devices and the pervasive nature of social media. By recognizing the influence of technology, we can take intentional steps to create space for silence in our lives.

The Rise of Silent Spaces

As awareness of the benefits of silence grows, there has been a rise in the creation of silent spaces. From quiet rooms in public libraries to silent retreats and meditation centers, these spaces provide sanctuaries where individuals can escape the noise and reconnect with themselves. This section explores the development of silent spaces and their significance in modern society.

Digital Detox: Disconnecting to Reconnect

A digital detox involves taking a break from digital devices to reconnect with the present moment. This section discusses the benefits of disconnecting from technology and the importance of creating tech-free zones and moments in daily life. By setting boundaries with our digital devices, we can cultivate a sense of peace and quietude.

Case Study: The Benefits of a Digital Detox

Consider the story of James, a marketing professional who felt overwhelmed by the constant demands of his digital life. He decided to embark on a digital detox, setting aside one day each week to disconnect from all digital devices. During these tech-free days, James spent time in nature, read books, and practiced mindfulness. He found that these periods of silence and disconnection allowed him to recharge and approach his work with renewed focus and creativity. James' experience highlights the benefits of a digital detox and the importance of creating space for silence in a technology-driven world.

The Importance of Quiet Moments

Quiet moments allow us to recharge and reflect, fostering a sense of balance and well-being. This section explores the importance of incorporating quiet moments into our daily routines, such as taking short breaks for mindfulness, enjoying silent walks, and practicing meditation. By making space for quiet moments, we can enhance our mental and emotional health.

Societal Shifts Towards Valuing Silence

CHAPTER 11: SILENCE IN MODERN SOCIETY

As the awareness of the benefits of silence grows, there is a societal shift towards valuing quietude. This section explores how communities and organizations are embracing silence, from creating quiet zones in public spaces to promoting mindfulness in schools and workplaces. By recognizing the importance of silence, we can create a more balanced and mindful society.

13

Chapter 12: The Future of Silence

As we move forward, the practice of silence and stillness will continue to evolve. This chapter speculates on the future of these practices and how they might shape future generations and societies. We discuss the potential for a more mindful and connected world through the power of quietude.

The Evolving Role of Silence

Silence has always been a part of human life, but its role is continually evolving. This section explores how the concept of silence might change in the future, particularly in response to technological advancements and societal shifts. We discuss how the growing awareness of the benefits of silence could lead to new practices and innovations that prioritize quietude.

Technological Innovations and Silence

Emerging technologies have the potential to both challenge and support the practice of silence. This section examines how future technologies, such as virtual reality and artificial intelligence, might be used to create immersive experiences of silence and stillness. We also discuss the importance

CHAPTER 12: THE FUTURE OF SILENCE

of balancing technological advancements with the need for quiet moments.

The Impact of Silence on Future Generations

As the benefits of silence become more widely recognized, there is potential for future generations to grow up in environments that value and prioritize quietude. This section explores how the practice of silence might be integrated into education, parenting, and community-building, fostering a culture that embraces stillness and reflection.

Case Study: A Future-Oriented Silent Community

Imagine a community designed with silence in mind. This section presents a hypothetical case study of a future-oriented community that incorporates quiet spaces, silent retreats, and mindful practices into daily life. We explore how such a community might thrive, highlighting the potential benefits for mental and emotional well-being.

The Role of Silence in Environmental Sustainability

Silence and stillness are deeply connected to our natural environment. This section discusses how the practice of silence can promote environmental awareness and sustainability. By creating quiet spaces and fostering a connection with nature, we can cultivate a deeper appreciation for the environment and inspire actions that support its preservation.

Envisioning a Mindful and Connected World

The future holds endless possibilities for the practice of silence and stillness. This section envisions a world where quietude is embraced and valued for its profound impact on our lives. We speculate on how these practices might shape our societies, relationships, and individual well-being, creating a more mindful and connected world.

14

Chapter 13: 10 reflective exercises that can help you cultivate silence, stillness, and deeper connections with yourself and others

1. Morning Meditation: Begin each day with a 10-minute meditation. Focus on your breath, letting go of thoughts as they arise. This practice can set a calm and mindful tone for the rest of your day.

2. Silent Nature Walks: Take a walk in a natural setting without any distractions. Pay attention to the sounds, sights, and sensations around you. Use this time to reflect on your connection to nature and the present moment.

3. Gratitude Journaling: At the end of each day, write down three things you are grateful for. Reflect on how these positive aspects of your life make you feel and how they contribute to your overall well-being.

4. Mindful Eating: Practice eating a meal in silence, paying full attention to the taste, texture, and aroma of your food. Reflect on how mindful eating

CHAPTER 13: 10 REFLECTIVE EXERCISES THAT CAN HELP YOU...

changes your experience and enhances your appreciation for the meal.

5. Body Scan Meditation: Lie down in a comfortable position and perform a body scan meditation, focusing on each part of your body from head to toe. Reflect on any areas of tension or relaxation and how they relate to your emotions and thoughts.

6. Reflective Reading: Choose a book or article that resonates with you and read it in a quiet space. After reading, spend some time reflecting on the themes and insights, and how they apply to your life.

7. Silent Journaling: Set aside time each week for silent journaling. Write about your thoughts, feelings, and experiences without any distractions. Reflect on any patterns or insights that emerge from your writing.

8. Visualization Exercises: Practice visualization by imagining a peaceful and serene place. Spend time visualizing the details of this place and reflect on the feelings of calm and relaxation it brings.

9. Mindful Breathing: Throughout the day, take a few moments to practice mindful breathing. Focus on your breath, noticing the inhale and exhale. Reflect on how this practice helps you stay grounded and present.

10. Silent Retreats: Plan a short silent retreat, whether it's a weekend or just a day. Disconnect from technology and spend the time in quiet reflection, meditation, and nature. Reflect on the insights and peace that arise from this extended period of silence.

These exercises can help you cultivate a deeper sense of peace, clarity, and connection with yourself and others. Incorporate them into your routine to experience the transformative power of silence and stillness.

www.ingramcontent.com/pod-product-compliance
Lightning Source LLC
LaVergne TN
LVHW020457080526
838202LV00057B/5997